Old MARYHILL

by

Guthrie Hutton

Maryhill owes its origins to the Forth and Clyde Canal and before the village name became fixed it was known as Drydock, The Dock or Kelvindock. The clutter of boats here occupies the basin and boatyard beside the dry dock, which is still known as Kelvin Dock. The Maryhill Fleet, the name given to some of these assorted craft, sailed for the last time in the spring of 1962, the canal closed at the end of the year.

© Copyright 1994 Guthrie Hutton
First Published in the United Kingdom 1994
By Richard Stenlake Publishing, Ochiltree Sawmill, The Lade, Ochiltree, Ayrshire KA18 2NX
Telephone 01290 700266
ISBN 1-872074-54-5

DETACHMENT OF GLASGOW LAMP LIGHTERS (MARYHILL DIVISION), 1905.

Everyone knew everyone else in old Maryhill, so when the leerie trudged up and down tenement stairs to light the close lamps he would bang on doors to wake the slumbering occupants for their early shifts at work (so who needs an alarm call when you've got gas lighting?). A pend near the Punch Bowl pub was known as gaslighters pend, although this photograph appears to have been taken when the lamp lighters were based across the road at the Burgh Hall buildings.

INTRODUCTION

Maryhill, dear Maryhill, I lo'e your sunlit braes,
Where aften times, lang syne, oor mithers bleached oor weel worn claes;
And in the gloamin's weird licht, I sadly sit and mourn,
When I think upo' the wee well and Wyndford's singin' burn.

Hew Hill, the laird of Gairbraid, had no male heir and so he left the estate to his daughter, Mary. She married Robert Graham in 1763, but they had no income from trade or commerce and had to make what they could from the estate. Coal mines proved to be wet and unprofitable and their real estate ventures are best known for an acre of ground they did not sell. It is still known as Acre. No doubt they would have continued with the struggle, but on the 8th March 1768 Parliament approved the cutting of the Forth and Clyde Canal through their estate; they had hit the jackpot!

The canal reached Stockingfield in 1775 and Hamilton Hill by 1777, but the Canal Company had run out of money and work stopped for eight years. The Government granted funds from forfeited Jacobite estates to start it again and the crossing of the River Kelvin became the focus for massive construction activity. Five locks, the great Kelvin aqueduct and, between two of the locks, a dry dock and boatyard were built. A village too began to grow up and the Grahams feued more land for its development attaching a condition that was to immortalise the heiress of Gairbraid; it was to be 'in all times called the town of Mary Hill'.

The first industries of milling, calico printing and papermaking were established beside the River Kelvin, but the canal brought new industries; boatbuilding, sawmilling and ironfounding. Later, in the railway age, chemical industries, paint, rubber and glass making became established in the area too.

Most of the early development was around Kelvindock. A lot of pubs (one to every 59 inhabitants) developed too and the area gained a reputation for drunken lawlessness. Mary Hill's grandson, John Dunlop, an unpopular absentee landlord, was appalled by what he saw on his visits to the area and in 1829 founded the first Temperance Society in Britain, in Maryhill; now there's a claim to fame! Into this unruly neighbourhood in the 1850's streamed a huge population of itinerant navvies to build the Glasgow, Dumbarton and Helensburgh Railway and lay the water pipes from Loch Katrine down Maryhill Road to Glasgow. A bad situation had got infinitely worse and after appealing unsuccessfully to Glasgow for help, the people of Maryhill sought police burgh status to clean up the town. It was granted in 1856.

There was still very little development along the main road into Glasgow, which wasn't called Maryhill Road until much later, but gradually the fields and estates started to disappear under factories and houses as Maryhill and Glasgow grew towards each other. The process accelerated towards the end of the century so that when the burgh was absorbed into Glasgow in 1891 tenements were being built along the length of Maryhill Road and in adjoining streets. Now, many of those tenements have been demolished, the trams that once ran through Maryhill and on to Milngavie have disappeared, the canal is closed and much of the industry has gone. But despite these changes Maryhill has never lost its identity or spirit and a new Maryhill is now emerging from the demolition sites of the 1960's and 70's to ensure that the twenty first century will not forget the name of a remarkable eighteenth century lady.

Guthrie Hutton, September 1994.

DAWSHOLM MILL LADE, MARYHILL.

Before the canal came to Maryhill, industry was concentrated beside the River Kelvin. Mills used the river so heavily that the canal builders had to construct a compensation reservoir in the Kilpatrick Hills to feed more water into the river when there was insufficient flow to drive the mills. It is still possible to see where the Dawsholm Mill dam was, despite it being deliberately breached in the 1940's. A substantial spur protrudes from the north bank and the remains of the sluices and entry to the mill lade can be found in the undergrowth beside Dawsholm Park. Before it was destroyed, youngsters used to swim in the mill pond, apparently less concerned about the presence of leeches than Humphrey Bogart was in the 'African Queen'!

Kelvin Bridge,
Dawsholm, Maryhill.

Dalsholm Mill was originally a grain mill, but William Macarthur started papermaking there in 1783. For the first fifty years or so the paper was hand made until superseded by machine made paper. The Macarthur family sold the mill in 1878 and, despite a variety of owners, it continued to make paper up to 1970 when it was closed. There was also an adjacent snuff mill up to the mid-nineteenth century. The mill has been demolished and the site landscaped as an extension to Dawsholm Park, but the column bases for the building that sat in the river can still be seen and there is a gate in Dalsholm Road with a stone plaque on it that simply says 'Dalsholm' - local people could never agree on what the correct spelling should be! The great cliff on the opposite bank of the Kelvin is known as Belcraig and at one time miners tunnelled into it for coal.

Garscube House.

Caledonia Series 91

Great estates and country houses were typical of the Maryhill landscape up to the late nineteenth century when industry and associated housing swallowed up most of these 'gentleman's seats'. Sir Archibald Islay Campbell of Succoth's 72 acre Garscube Estate survived on the fringe of modern Maryhill until 1921 when part of it was made into Dawsholm Park, houses were built on a corner at Canniesburn and the remainder was purchased by the University of Glasgow for use as their Vet College and student halls of Residence. Garscube House, which had been built in 1827, succumbed to dry rot in 1954 and was demolished. The low terrace walls to the front and the retaining wall rising out of the River Kelvin still survive along with an ornamental stone bridge that carried the main drive over the River Kelvin, to Maryhill Road.

BAILLIE CLELLAND'S HOUSE, MARYHILL.

Another of the great houses was Bonville, built by Andrew Walker in 1810. Its last owner was Sir Charles Cleland who became the youngest Town Councillor of Glasgow, at the age of 24, when Maryhill became part of Glasgow in 1891 (and a Conservative too!). Ten years later he was a senior magistrate and later became the first chairman of the Education Authority of Glasgow, a post he held for ten years. He was also acting chairman of the British Film Institute for a time in the 1930's. He died in 1941. The house was demolished in 1948 and the Church of the Immaculate Conception was built on the site to replace the original church which had stood in Maryhill Road, between Kilmun Street and Duncruin Street since 1851. The new A frame church was highly distinctive, but sadly it was also structurally unsound and has itself now been replaced by a more modest structure.

The first Maryhill railway station was at the western end of Maryhill Road on the Glasgow, Dumbarton and Helensburgh Railway which was opened in 1858. A branch was later built through Summerston to the Kelvin Valley. The line served the last coal mine in the area and these slow moving coal trains were looked on as a ready source of 'free' coal by local boys. When British Railways took over the line they changed the station name to Maryhill Park. Then, on 2nd October 1961, with increasing numbers of cars from Bearsden and Milngavie hurtling past to clog up Maryhill Road, they closed the station, although unscheduled trains continued to take workers from Maryhill to the Singer Sewing Machine works in Clydebank, until it too was closed. The station was re-opened on 3rd December 1993, reverting to its original name of Maryhill. But the cars still clog up Maryhill Road!

PARISH CHURCH, MARYHILL.

Maryhill Old Parish Church was built as a Chapel of Ease in 1824. It is unusual amongst city churches in having a graveyard and the memorials to farmers and industrial families are a fascinating illustration of Maryhill's position on the edge of both city and country. There is also an interesting memorial to an industrial martyr; a young striker killed during a dispute in the print industry. The graves of people who died during outbreaks of cholera in 1831 and 1832 were also discovered when the wall at the front of the churchyard was moved back to widen Maryhill Road. The first minister of the church was Robert MacNair Wilson, but during 'the disruption' of 1843 he left the established church, with most of the congregation, to set up the Free Church. This view of the now closed and derelict church was radically altered in 1924 when a grand 'centenary' frontage was added to the simple, austere original.

Maryhill Bowling Club is the oldest surviving sporting club in the area (the oldest was the Kelvindock Curling Club which played on a flooded quarry). It was formed in 1861 and the green was ready for use on 27th July. The first club match against Killermont was followed by matches against Partick Artisans and Springburn. Since then, club members have won numerous Glasgow Bowling Association championship and cup competitions. The clubhouse has grown from a simple, shed like, pavilion to the present modern structure. The imposing building behind the green here was built in 1883 as a tram depot and stables for the Glasgow Tram and Omnibus Company, the private company that operated tram services in Glasgow before the Corporation of Glasgow started their own service in 1894. The building was later used by International Paints (Scotland) Ltd., also known as Hamilton's Paint Works.

Kilmun Street was originally called Argyle Street, but the name was changed in 1930. The street was badly damaged during a German air raid on the night of 14th March 1941 when a land mine exploded into the backs of some houses. One hundred and seven people were killed in a tragedy compounded by its futility; the main target in Maryhill was MacLellan's Rubber Works a mile away. The Old Parish Church commemorated the bombing in a stained glass window, an unusual wartime memorial to civilian losses. Saint Mary's School in Duncruin Street, which was being used as an air raid shelter, was also badly damaged. The top two floors were beyond repair and demolished, leaving a truncated building seen here in 1950 from Kilmun Street, through the gap left by the demolished houses. Since then the whole site, including adjacent property in Maryhill Road has been cleared and a new school built.

The name of Maryhill Road was not adopted until 1922. Before that different sections of the road had different names and the section from the city boundary to the canal aqueduct was called Main Street. The original tram terminus was at the top of Main Street, the Glasgow Tram and Omnibus Company depot was to the right and the Corporation's new depot to the left. It was later extended behind the tenement where Gairbraid Farm was knocked down to make way for it. Behind the tram two famous pubs faced each other across the road; to the left was Cloughleys (now the Ram's Head) which only sold beer, while to the right was the First and Last which sold 'Old Mac' whisky from barrels. To the right of the tram the double gabled Royal Bank building still exists, but all of the two storey buildings have been demolished. The tram line was extended to the city boundary at Killermont Bridge by 1911 and to Milngavie in the 1920's.

12

In the 1890's the Partick and Maryhill Press regularly reported on 'cursing and swearing' and 'riotous behaviour' in Main Street and 'another Main Street square' meant that two more gladiators had been nicked for 'quarreling and fighting'; to add to the colour, the Catholic Priest armed with a shillelagh, and the Episcopal Curate, patrolled it together to drag hard drinking husbands out of the pubs and send them back to their families. On the left of this view of Main Street is the distinctive tenement known as Maryhill Cross which replaced a row of whitewashed, thatched roofed shops and houses in 1900. Beyond the tenement block on the other side of the road was a stair that led between the buildings to the terraced high ground behind. It was known to generations of Maryhill youngsters as the Redan (the name of a Russian fortress stormed by the British during the Crimean War). A pub perpetuates the name.

'Tam' Morrison, from Falkirk, set up the boatbuilding yard at Kelvin Dock. It built barges known as scows or lighters, sea going lighters (gabbarts) and sailing smacks. Tam's grandson in law David Swan (who was to become the first provost of Maryhill) and his brother William Swan took over the yard and set up a sawmill around 1842. In 1857 they launched a boat that started a folk legend. She was an iron hulled, steam powered, screw propelled canal lighter called the Glasgow and she is regarded as the first ever puffer. Under the later ownership of the McNicoll brothers, the yard continued to build puffers, the last two being the Logan and the Kype, seen here being launched on 7th February 1921. The Swans' house 'Collina' overlooked the canal basin from the hill now occupied by the Collina Street flats and the housing scheme known, after a 1930's pop song, as 'sleepy valley'.

Below 'Collina', next to the top lock, was a spelter works (spelter is a copper/zinc alloy which was widely used in the 19th century for joining other metals). The building was later used by the Kelvindock Chemical Company. A canal hostelry on the other side of the canal, next to the second lock down, had to remain open for genuine travellers 24 hours a day and many devious ploys were used by non-travelling Maryhill folk to obtain drink from it. The locks were a centre of activity for weans too. They helped to open and close the lock gates for boats, like this fishing boat, and, if they were lucky, the crew would then let them sail on to the next lock or bridge. Some tell of long journeys and having to find their way home from far flung foreign places, like Clydebank! The locks, dock and aqueduct are the finest collection of canal structures in Scotland and a heritage centre beside them would put Maryhill on the tourist trail!

These little engines operated at the Dawsholm Gas Works which Glasgow Corporation started to build in 1871. The works had an initial capacity of three million cubic feet a day, increased to eight million in 1883 and increased again in 1891 when the Corporation bought the Temple Gas Works of the Partick, Hillhead and Maryhill Gas Company. The two works were linked by a tunnel under the canal and by 1896 the joint plant capacity was 17 million cubic feet a day. Further increases in capacity were achieved when the retorts at Dawsholm were replaced in 1911. Coke was distributed into a riddling machine, railway waggons or storage by a 200 foot long jib transporter crane, but only a simple shute was needed to supply people who took their steamie pram to the Gas Works to have it filled with coke, in exchange for a token issued at the gatehouse.

The Gas Works were built on the site of Dawsholm Printworks, the oldest linen and calico printworks in Scotland. They were set up in the 1750's by William Stirling and Company who later moved to larger works in the Vale of Leven. The Dawsholm works were taken over by a William Robb and for the next hundred years they remained in more or less continuous operation, surviving a succession of owners and a couple of bankruptcies until John Finlay and Company sold the site to Glasgow Corporation for the Gas Works. William Robb built a row of workers houses in Bridge Street (now Bantaskin Street), which is shown on an early map as 'Botany Feu's'. Behind it, another row of houses known as the 'Cages' faced what was Kelvin Street. The origin of these curious names is unknown but the map appears to be the first use of the name Botany by which the area is still known.

17

The names could have been derived from the print industry, but in the absence of any other explanation, colourful theories abound. The first convicts were shipped to Australia in 1787 at the same time as the Kelvin Aqueduct was being built and either: convicts were transported from here, or convicts were used to build the aqueduct before they were transported, or hewing and shifting stone on the construction site just seemed like penal servitude to canal navvies. Did navvy humour liken it to Botany Bay? Nobody knows, and the real origin of the name is probably much simpler and lost forever. This view looking across Kelvin Dock shows the Botany with the Gas Works in the background. There was a beeswax and taper works in the Botany, an ironmoulders blacking factory, in what had originally been the Maryhill Printworks, and Simpson's model lodging house where a ha'penny would buy two nights accommodation.

A year after the formation of the Burgh of Maryhill its administrative buildings were opened at the corner of Fingal Street and Maryhill Road. The accommodation included a flat on the upper floor for the Superintendent of Police and a court room, for Police Court trials. The barred window seen here in the Fingal Street gable no doubt indicates where the court's customers waited for their moment of glory. The building continued to be occupied after it was superseded by the Burgh Halls in 1878, the last resident being a Doctor Crighton, who was known as the 'Police Doctor'. The building was demolished in 1949 when this picture was taken. On the opposite corner of Fingal Street is the Kelvin Dock pub, the last remnant of a tenement block (the one on the right on page 15) and the last visible reminder of the old village name before it became known as Maryhill.

Barges from Drumpellier, near Coatbridge, delivered coal direct to the Maryhill coal wharf; just above the top lock. The coal ree (coal yard) occupied the strip of ground, between the canal and Maryhill Road to the south of the building that is now the White House pub. It not only served Maryhill, but sent cart loads of coal to Milngavie too. The ree was closed at the end of the First World War. Paterson & Stewart, motor engineers, took over the site and set up this garage. They also operated a taxi service with a driver who had a reputation for being uniformly untidy, regardless of who his customers were. The building has gone, but taxis still operate from the site. The White House pub was originally built by Andrew Walker of Bonville as a grocery and public house and is one of the few buildings remaining from the old village. The perversely named 'valley' can be seen on the hill behind the garage.

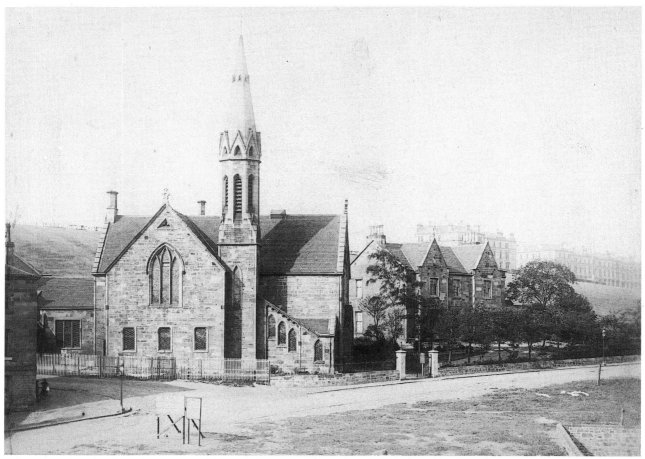

During 'The Disruption', the schism between the Established and Free Churches in 1843, most of the congregation of the Old Parish Church left with their minister Robert MacNair Wilson to form the Free Church. They quickly found they had no place to worship, but, since nobody was using the old building, they moved back in. They were evicted four years later and again found themselves without a church, but the following Sunday met in the Kelvin Dock sawmill. It became known as 'Maryhill Cathedral' (see inside front cover) because services continued there, with planks for seats, until the new church, Maryhill High, was built. It is seen here from the canal bank, before the view was obscured by tenements in Maryhill Road. It sits on the corner of what is now Aray Street and Sandbank Street, which used to be called Church Street; hardly surprising with both Maryhill High and Saint George's Episcopal Church in it.

When the first aqueduct was built over what is now Maryhill Road no one knew how to build a skew bridge and so the road was cut and re-aligned straight through the arch. A new section of road was built beside the canal which re-joined the old road near Kelvin Dock. The cut off section of old road is now Aray Street, Sandbank Street was originally just a link from it to the new road. The original aqueduct was like the one in Lochburn Road. It's small arch created problems for laying the water pipes down Maryhill Road and was a barrier to extending the new tramway system and so this new aqueduct was built in 1881. To the left of the aqueduct, in this picture from 1958, is a circular valve house and beside it a pumping station used to supply water to Gilsochill. The retaining wall on the right was built to support the canal embankment when Maryhill Road was widened, but a house and some cottages had to be knocked down to make way for it.

The new aqueduct was built on the city side of the old one and the line of the canal altered so that it went over it through a sharper S bend. The canal apparently burst while this was being done and the water flooded Maryhill Road and flowed down Kelvindale Road to the River Kelvin. During the emergency, Captain Anderson, the Chief of Police, is said to have directed operations from an upturned kitchen table. For many old Maryhill people the 'Pen Bridge', as the aqueduct was known, was the old village limit and so this 1958 view from the top of the aqueduct would not, to them, have been of Maryhill. The two and three storey buildings on the left have since been demolished, although the tenements have all survived along with the Library, in the top right corner of the picture with the Punch Bowl pub beside it. The 29 tram service was replaced by the 61 bus in 1961.

Maryhill United Presbyterian Church was opened on 1st May 1859. The congregation had worshipped for some time in the Odd-fellows Hall at the corner of Main Street and Walker Street (now Glencloy Street) and had looked at other sites before deciding to build their new church beside the canal aqueduct. It was built without a spire, to save money. The manse on the left of the picture and the hall on the right were added later. When the canal was re-aligned over the new aqueduct the church received £400 in compensation for the loss of the land. In 1900 the church changed its name to Gairbraid to distinguish it from Maryhill High when the United Presbyterian and the United Free Churches joined together. Another name change was of course Maryhill Road, in the foreground, which before 1922 was called Wyndford Street between the canal aqueduct and Shawpark Street.

The first library in Maryhill was opened in 1823 with 93 books. It was supported by the donations of benefactors, subscriptions of members and the proceeds of lectures. By 1850 it had over 600 books and had been located in a number of buildings. The present Library was opened in 1905 with this general reading room, seen here in 1907, and separate reading rooms for ladies, girls and boys. It was one of fourteen local public libraries in Glasgow to benefit from a gift to Glasgow Corporation of £100,000 from Andrew Carnegie. As a small boy Carnegie had gone to America with his parents, sailing from the Broomielaw. He had always felt an affinity with this last bit of Scotland and he made the gift to commemorate the important part Glasgow had played in his life. When the library opened it had over 10,000 books, took in 114 newspapers and periodicals and could accommodate over 300 readers.

Mary Hill's Gairbraid House was on high ground overlooking the Kelvin, at the end of a long avenue, but as the burgh developed, industry gradually overwhelmed it. The Kelvindale Laundry almost surrounded it, a dye works was built opposite and Dawsholm locomotive works and railway yards were below it. All that now remains is the name of Gairbraid Avenue. The Burgh Halls, on the right of the picture, were built on the corner of Gairbraid Avenue and Wyndford Street (Maryhill Road) and opened on 24th April 1878. Set into the windows of the main hall were twenty stained glass panels, now kept in the People's Palace Museum on Glasgow Green. They are unusual in that they depict the industries and occupations of the area, rather than imaginary scenes, and the wide variety of industries and occupations in Maryhill makes them a unique record of nineteenth century Scottish life.

The centre of Maryhill effectively moved south with the Burgh Halls. The Police, Fire Brigade and Lamp Lighters were all based there the baths and wash houses, were built next door on the corner of Burnhouse Street. The function of the Burgh Halls came to an end when Maryhill was absorbed into Glasgow but the Police continued to use the building until they moved into new premises across Maryhill Road. This now sad and neglected symbol of the pride Maryhill once had in itself is still searching for a new role, while across Gairbrad Avenue, Glasgow District Council have built a graceless, inelegant office block for the Housing Department, in marked contrast to the old Burgh Halls. The tenement on the right, on the corner of Lochburn Road, replaced a row of cottages that extended down Maryhill Road with Lochburn Road running round behind them. Opposite the cottages was a blacksmiths shop.

Maryhill Harriers was formed in 1888 and became one of the foremost clubs in Scotland. Its heyday was between 1927 and 1932 when it won the Scottish National Team Cross Country Championships six years in succession, a feat only recently equalled and not yet beaten. One of the mainstays of the club at that time was Duncan 'Dunkie' Wright who won marathon gold for Scotland at the inaugural Empire (now Commonwealth) Games in 1930, at Hamilton, Ontario. He also came fourth in the Olympic marathon at Los Angeles in 1932, but was lucky to be there because Donald Robertson, another Maryhill Harrier, had been selected for the Games but had to withdraw, because he could not afford to lose six weeks wages; amateur athletes were indeed amateur in those days. For many years the club used the baths as a base and this picture shows some of the runners there in 1940.

Lochburn Home, on the right here, was one of the largest Magdalene Institutions in Scotland. It was a gaunt, grey building, somehow appropriate for its Dickensian purpose of the 'repression of vice', 'rescue of fallen women' and 'protection of women and girls being led astray'. The girls sent to the Magdalene 'for their own good' worked long hours, for no pay, providing a laundry service to hospitals and other institutions. They were locked up, sometimes for years, the food was poor, magazines were censored for morally corrupting material and in September 1958 the girls at Lochburn had had enough. They broke out, twice within a few days and were chased by Police all over Maryhill. The institution didn't last long after that and the building was demolished in 1961. The Girl's Industrial School on the left was also used as a school for deaf children.

The Roxy, opened in 1930, was one of five cinemas in Maryhill Road. It was built on the site of the earlier Maryhill Picture House and took its name from the great Roxy cinema in Chicago, the largest picture house in the world. Like its namesake it was huge, seating 2270. The price of a Saturday matinee was a penny and even a jeely jar (worth a penny) was accepted as currency, but not everyone paid. When the lights went out youngsters already inside would rush to the toilets - not because they were caught short, but because they could open an exit door beside the toilets to let in their mates who were waiting outside in the lane. Entertainment at the Roxy transcended mere movies and Thursday night was talent night when local people could perform between pictures. The Roxy Café was next door to the cinema which closed in 1962 and was demolished.

Saint Mary's School annexe was built in 1933 on a site diagonally across Maryhill Road from the Roxy and a new hut was added in 1950. The Castle Brewery occupied the site before the school and before that it was the Wyndford Mill where Robert Jeffrey and Sons used steam powered looms for weaving linen. It is now the site of the Police Station. Beside it, to the south, was a two storey building that was the local Conservative Party rooms, their large hall popular for receptions and dances. Later, when the building became a pub it was called the Politician, a name that neatly recalled the previous occupants and the name of the 'Whisky Galore' ship. The building is now also used by an Indian restaurant. Behind the school, in this picture from 1950, are the tenements of Shawpark and Craigmont Streets and the double pitched roofed building on the left was part of the Maryhill Iron Works.

Maryhill Barracks was built on the Garrioch Estate, then on the fringe of the city, to replace the old and unsuitable Gallowgate barracks. The city magistrates had requested the replacement because they were worried about possible riot and disorder amongst the large, and mostly immigrant, industrial labouring population. Building began in 1869, but a dispute with the contractor delayed their completion by Royal Engineers until 1876. They were designed for a regiment of infantry, but the plans were extended to include artillery and cavalry too. The picture on these two pages shows an inspection of the 1st Battalion, the Royal Scots Fusiliers by the Duke of Cambridge in 1891; many famous regiments used the barracks before 1920 when they became the depot for, and closely identified with, the Highland Light Infantry. Before that, the only unit of the HLI to have been stationed there, was the 74th Highlanders in 1880/81.

The barracks were not built for comfort, but the first thing every old soldier recalls about them are the plumbing arrangements. No doubt the idea of putting washing facilities on balconies exposed to the elements was to heed lessons in personal hygiene learned in the Crimean War, but while such a design might have been suitable in a warm climate, in a Maryhill winter, pipes and soldiers both froze. The great barrack blocks on the left housed a platoon to each room; the soldiers presented their kit for inspection by lining it up on their bunks with a piece of string stretched between marks at each end of the barrack room walls. The N.C.O's and Sergeants had smaller rooms while the officers quarters were in this smaller building. The HLI vacated the barracks in 1958 and moved to Ayr where they amalgamated with the Royal Scots Fusiliers to become the Royal Highland Fusiliers.

Station and Barracks, Maryhill, Glasgow

Glasgow Corporation demolished the barracks when the Army left and built the Wyndford Housing Estate on the site. The guard house was kept as an estate office and the perimeter wall was also left surrounding the estate. It is a source of great local pride and when it was threatened by proposals to re-align this junction of Garrioch Road with Maryhill Road the estate residents sprang to its defence with an alacrity that would have gladdened the hearts of the old soldiers. Across Garrioch Road, the Maryhill Shopping Mall has been built on the site of the station shown on the cover of the book and seen here as it was at street level. Leaving Maryhill, the railway went under Maryhill Road, below the canal and through Tamshill tunnel to Possil. The bridge that took it under the road can be seen in the foreground, as can the roof and chimney of a building that was used for about sixty years by the builders James Muirhead and Sons.

34

The picture on the previous page was taken from a gable window of the tenement on the extreme left of this picture of the Glasgow Soldier's Home. The home was a comfortable alternative for soldiers who wanted to escape the rigours of barrack life, when they had some time off. A newly wed soldier, unable to afford the honeymoon suite at a city hotel, could get a room for himself and his bride at the Home. When the Home closed the building was used first by the Red Cross and then as a Trade Union centre. It is now a night club, but the initials GSH are still carved in a stone panel above the door. Other military associations with Maryhill are beginning to fade too. The Elephant and Bugle pub, on the site of the Roxy, which took its name from the badge of the HLI, is now just called the Bugle and another pub, the HLI, at the corner of Maryhill Road and Kelvinside Avenue has been demolished.

Construction of Bryant and May's Empire Works in Shuna Street was started in 1918 and, despite a scarcity of labour and difficulty in obtaining suitable materials under war-time conditions, the factory was ready to start production in May 1919. A year later the main building was extended to twice its original size and further extensions were made to accommodate more efficient wood drying chambers, case making room and a new mixing house. With the factory on high ground water pressure was low and so a water tower was needed to increase it. The tower provided an ideal advertising opportunity and in 1922 gave a David MacKinlay his moment of glory when he climbed up the flagpole, 100 feet above the ground, to paint it; not perhaps in the spirit of today's emphasis on health and safety at work, but a talking point at the time.

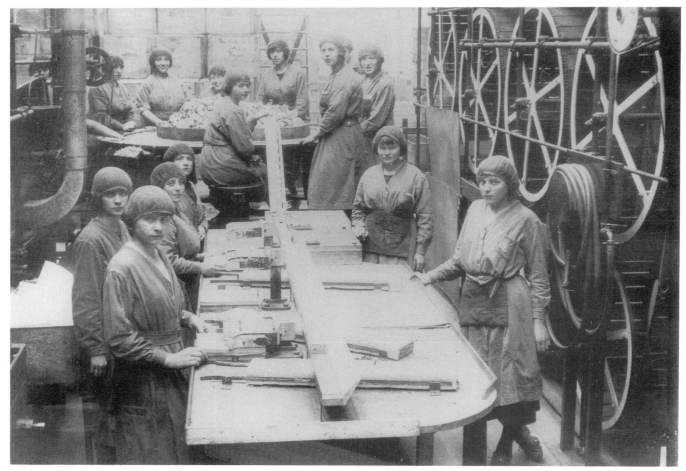

In other ways Bryant and May looked after their employees well. They had a dental surgery, to combat the danger of phosphorus necrosis (or phossy jaw), a hazard in the match making industry where the jaw bone was rotted by the fumes of yellow phosphorus. They also introduced a co-partnership share scheme and a range of welfare arrangements for their employees. These little match girls of Maryhill had a hockey pitch, tennis courts, swings and see-saw in the factory grounds for recreation, while their male colleagues had a quoiting pitch beside the canal or played football. In this 1920's picture the girls are working on the production line for Puck matches, but the factory later made Scottish Bluebell matches which became closely identified with the Scottish market and Swan Vestas Despite being earmarked for modernisation in the 1960's the factory closed in 1981.

Maryhill's tenement streets were devoid of the usual indications of changing seasons and so it wasn't the green trees or singing birds that heralded summer, it was the cheery sound of the Gipsy Queen's hooter as she started her season of pleasure cruises. The first pleasure steamers on the canal, the Fairy Queen and the May Queen, had been taken off before the First World War, but the Gipsy Queen continued to sail from Port Dundas to Criagmarloch, near Kilsyth, up to the start of the Second World War. She is seen here in 1905, her first season on the canal, heading for the countryside past Ruchill Bridge and leaving behind all the industrial grime and noise that typified the factories beside the canal. On the left is the Maryhill Iron Works while on the right are the Ruchill Iron Works and the white lead factory of Alexander Ferguson's Glasgow Lead and Colour Works.

The small wooden bridges over the Forth and Clyde Canal were known as bascule bridges, from a French word meaning see-saw. When the canal closed on 1st January 1963 this one at Ruchill Street was replaced by an ugly drowned culvert which itself has recently been replaced by a new bridge. The two storey building on the left of this picture was built in 1874 for Alexander Ferguson's Glasgow Lead and Colour Works, which had buildings on both sides of Ruchill Street (as seen on the right of the previous page), the large building behind it is part of MacLellan's Rubber Works. The semi-rural nature of the area at the time made it an ideal location for factories that gave off unpleasant fumes! Ruchill Street Bridge was also known as Jean's Brig, while the next bridge, Firhill Bridge, was known to a generation of youngsters as where the bridge keeper Jock Young or 'Jock the Briggie' lived and worked.

George MacLellan left the family business early in 1871. He set up an engineering merchandising business as a front to disguise his real intention; the manufacture of India-rubber goods. He quickly acquired a red brick factory beside the Ruchill canal bridge and by 1873 the Glasgow Rubber Works was in production. In 1879 he went on a world tour to promote the firm and won the gold medal at the Sydney exhibition, but on the return journey he took ill and died in San Francisco: his 24 year old brother, Peter, took over and continued to run the firm for the next 52 years. The company made engine packing, carriage aprons, waterproof clothing, ground sheets, knapsacks, hoses, industrial belting, punched rubber mats etc. etc. and continually changed their product range to meet the demands of the day, which may explain why they are still in business on that original site.

South east of the barracks, on the remainder of the old Garrioch estate, are streets of more up-market red sandstone tenements that took the 'posh' name of North Kelvinside, to distinguish them from grubby old Maryhill. Garrioch Road seen here looking north-west linked the two. It was an old estate road that ran from Maryhill Road, with the barracks on one side and the railway on the other, before turning across the railway and becoming this residential street. The picture shows it, with the barracks in the background, at its junction with Garrioch Drive on the left and Shakespeare Street, which was also an old estate road, on the right. Opposite this corner at the foot of Shakespeare Street was an architectural curiosity, the half house. It's unique appearance gave rise to speculation in the 1930's press about its origins, but it was nothing more than a fanciful estate building

The School Board Educational Enquiry, set up after the introduction of compulsory education in 1872, showed that the extent of physical and mental disability amongst Glasgow children warranted a hospital school and East Park Cottage was bought for this purpose in 1874. To begin with only 30 children were admitted, but in 1903, after the building had been extended many times, the number of children at East Park Home had risen to 130. As housing and industry began to encroach on the semi-rural nature of the home a country branch was set up at Largs. During the Second World War it was used by the Maryhill children while East Park Home itself was used as an emergency hospital and later a wartime nursery. It resumed its work with disabled children after the war and links with Largs continued with the annual outing provided by Glasgow's taxi owners and drivers.

Children who were fit enough for school were taught in conventional class rooms, as here in 1904, but later there was a greater emphasis on craft work. The children also participated in Boy Scout, Girl Guide, Cub and Brownie activities. The medical and educational needs of the children have always been separated and dealt with by specialist staff. Some of the medical conditions treated when the Home started are thankfully rare now and wider care provision is available elsewhere. The Home's response to these changes has been to concentrate on the needs of profoundly mentally handicapped children and alter the old hospital ward style of accommodation to cater for their more individual requirements. East Park Home must be one of the most remarkable institutions to have survived from Victorian Glasgow and equally remarkably it still derives much of its income from charitable donations - go on, you can afford it!

The Star Cinema, later the New Star, was sandwiched between houses and extended into the back court. It was extended further into the back court in 1931 when the seating capacity was doubled to 1800. Movie makers were experimenting with wide screen pictures at the time and a wide screen was incorporated into the New Star. It came into its own in the 1950's when wide screen movies became popular, but too late to save the Star from closure in 1959. The building was used as a car showroom before being demolished. The Star's tin roof meant that the sound track could be heard 'halfway up Maryhill Road'. Movies were a big part of Maryhill life and A.E. Pickard, the wealthy, eccentric owner of the Seamore Cinema, near St. George's Cross (and many other cinemas in Glasgow) stood for Parliament in 1951 as the 'Independent Millionaire' candidate for Maryhill. He polled 356 votes and lost his deposit.

Before the wholesale demolition of tenement property in the 1960's and 70's, Maryhill Road was a varied and very busy shopping street with small shops lining both sides of the road. This tenement block between Vernon Street and Oran Street in the 1950's, is typical of the whole road. Campbell and Sons were butchers, Finlayson's sold confectionery, Guthrie was a hardware and china shop and there were two dairies, another butcher, Waddell's sausages, dyers and cleaners, a tobacconist, a grocer, dress shop, fancy goods, the City Bakeries, Boots the Chemist, Greenlees Easyphit Footwear, the Caberfeidh pub and many others. Everything, according to the sub-title of another small book on Maryhill Road, 'From a Needle to an Anchor'. And behind these facades children danced, sang and juggled in back court concerts to raise funds for East Park Home.

The staggered junction of Vernon Street on the left and Bilsland Drive on the right was only made into a cross roads and through route from Queen Margaret Drive when the streets between Maryhill Road and the top of Queen Margaret Drive were demolished in the 1960's and 70's. The trams had not been displaced by buses and cars when this picture was taken in the 1950's. Here a Coronation tram waits in Maryhill Road for Standard tram, No. 36 to turn out of Bilsland Drive on the old 'white' car, No.18, route from Springburn to Burnside. Bilsland Drive was created at the start of the tram age when a new aqueduct was built under the Forth and Clyde Canal. The Barber Shop in Bilsland Drive is still a hairdresser's, but Margaret Anderson's dress shop at 925 Maryhill Road has gone, along with McLeod's pub and the rest of the tenements on either side of Vernon Street.

Dunard Street, Maryhill.

The boundary of the old burgh runs diagonally across Maryhill Road at the foot of Dunard Street and so all the tenements on the right are technically in Glasgow and not Maryhill. Most of them have now gone, to be replaced by a play park, and large plant tubs block the street where the people are standing. But some things remain; there has been a doctor's surgery at the foot of the street since it was built, Dunard Street School is still there, just out of the picture on the left and Munn's pub in Maryhill Road has survived despite most of the building surrounding it being demolished. Above Maryhill Road, on the other side of the canal, is Murano Street, once famous for glass making. At one time a small cairn on the canal bank opposite the end of neighbouring Braeside Street commemorated a whisky smuggler who was stabbed in a fight with excise men near Agnes Street. He staggered across Maryhill Road and died beside the canal.

With the burgh boundary crossing Maryhill Road near Dunard Street, Queen's Cross is just outside old Maryhill, but it seems a more natural boundary than the long forgotten limit of an old estate. This view looking west up Maryhill Road is now much changed, the distant tenements on both sides of the road have been demolished as has the block on the extreme left between Kirkland Street and Bonawe Street. A video shop now occupies the Springbank Street corner site on the extreme right but a Police box that stood outside has, like Doctor Who's Tardis, disappeared to another world. Further up the block, the shop selling 'Ices' is where Cafe d'Jaconelli was opened in 1924. It became a Sunday evening 'must' for Maryhill teenagers who thronged in the 1950's to listen to the juke box, drink espresso coffee and chat each other up - anyone arriving after 6.00pm was left outside - singin' the blues!

48

The section of Maryhill Road from Queen's Cross down to Saint George's Cross used to be part of New City Road until the street name changes of 1922. The original highway that ran out of the city through Maryhill was known as the Garscube Road and the street leading away to the right of this picture is the last remaining section of it to bear the name (although it is better known locally as the Gaspipe Road!). In the centre of the picture is the Queen's Cross Church. It was designed by the famous Glasgow architect Charles Rennie MacIntosh in 1897 and, although no longer used as a church, is now the headquarters of the Charles Rennie MacIntosh Society. On the extreme left is a striped shop awning that would be a little inappropriate for today's occupant of the shop, the Co-op funeral services!

Ruchill Park is a remnant of Ruchill Estate, another old estate that became part of the old Burgh of Maryhill. This tranquil Edwardian scene shows the park near the gate leading to Firhill Road. The houses in Leny Street, on the right, are across Firhill Road from Benview Street just out of picture on the right. The Ben it has a view of is Ben Whitton, a natural hill, also sometimes known as Spion Kop after a famous Boer War battle. It was heightened around 1900 by the Superintendent of Parks James Whitton who had waste material from the building of Ruchill Hospital deposited on top of it. In the 1930's, a writer complained of never being able to enjoy the wonderful panoramic views from the top because of the smoky atmosphere and suggested that if Glasgow was ever cleared of its smoke pall, Ben Whitton would become a must for tourists. The smoke has now gone, but the tourists are not yet flocking to Ruchill Park.

Behind Leny Street, on the previous page, is Shaw and McInness' Firhill Ironworks, also, surprisingly, inside the Burgh boundary of old Maryhill. The original foundry was opened by James and John Shaw in 1846, but when John Shaw moved away in 1851 and James' brother in law Archibald McIness joined the firm, it took on the present name. It was known locally as a company that kept up with changes in the industry, which may explain why it has survived in a difficult world. There were a number of iron works beside the canal in Maryhill; the Kelvin Foundry between Lochburn Road and the canal, Maryhill Ironworks at Stockingfield and the large Springbank Works diagonally across the canal from Shaw and McInness. Like Tam Morrison of Kelvin Dock many of the early foundrymen came from Falkirk, as did the men who worked in the chemical industries, flitting to the west on puffers.

Although Firhill Stadium is outside the old burgh boundary and the team name reflects distant origins, Partick Thistle Football Club is one of the most enduring and best loved institutions in Maryhill. The club was formed in 1876 and after using various grounds in the Partick area, moved to Firhill in 1909. Despite concern at the move, Partick people still flocked to Maryhill to join locals in huge crowds for games against – Albion Rovers! In the 1950's Thistle were dubbed the Maryhill Magyars after the all conquering Hungarian teams of the time, but they are better known as the Jags, Firhill is still known for thrills and those jokes about the meat pies won't go away - just like the taste! If the weather was foggy and Thistle were losing, people in the houses on the right were accused of trying to affect the result by adding to the gloom with smoke from their fires. The houses thus became enshrined in football lore as the 'Firhill Lum'.

Thistle's greatest triumph was winning the Scottish Cup in 1921 with this team. In the final, Campbell was in goal, Crighton and Bulloch were full backs, half backs were Harris, Wilson and Borthwick, Kinloch, Johnstone and McMenemy were the inside forwards and on the wings were Blair and Salisbury. Blair, sitting on the ground on the left, scored the only goal of the game. The players wore dark blue jerseys with a white thistle, up to the early 1930's, when the distinctive red and yellow was adopted; a change apparently inspired by the strips of the West of Scotland Rugby Club. The colours emphasise the club's neutral place in the tribal hot house of Glasgow football and just to prove their neutrality, fifty years after beating Rangers in the Cup, their next major triumph was to beat Celtic in the League Cup final - nice!

MARYHILL JUNIORS F.C.

Maryhill Football Club is one of the oldest junior clubs in Scotland, formed in 1884. It moved to Lochburn Park in season 1897/98, on the site of Perrat's Quarry, where the Kelvindock Curling Club used to play. It was the first club to reach three consecutive finals of the Scottish Junior Cup, winning it in 1899/1900 and 1939/40 and being runners-up four times. The club has won the Central League Cup five times, the Glasgow Junior League three times and has been division two and division one champions of the Central League. Glasgow Rangers paid £20 and a corrugated iron fence (!) for the transfer of Davie Meiklejohn in the 1920's and other famous former players include Danny McGrain, Tommy Burns and Pat McCluskey of Celtic and Scotland. In this picture of the team in 1936 J Bone, standing second from the right, went on to play for Saint Johnstone.

Maryhill F.C. is commonly, but wrongly, known as Maryhill Juniors an error that possibly started as a way of distinguishing them from these one time local rivals, Maryhill Hibs, formed in 1924. The Hibs may have grown out of an earlier team called Maryhill Harp and indeed the name was changed to that later. The team played in the Scottish Junior League winning it twice and once being runners-up, but the club was wound up in the 1960's when the home ground at the top of Kilmun Street, was earmarked for housing. The picture from 1936 shows: Back row:- S Kelly (Treasurer), J Finnerton (Committee), S Hunter (Trainer), S Gowdie (Assistant Trainer), J McCann (Vice-President). Middle row:- J Hoy, P Murphy, D McClintock, A Galloway, J Kierna, W Wright (Captain). Front row:- A Clark (Secretary), John Beckest, H Harra, G Johnson, Joseph Beckest, H Boyle and M Kelly (President).

WHERE IS MARYHILL? I have taken the limits of Maryhill as being where the old burgh boundary was set in 1856, with a few limited exceptions. I hope this does not upset people who believe Maryhill extends beyond this line, but I had to stop somewhere!

BIBLIOGRAPHY

Alexander Thomson	Random Notes and Recollections of ... Maryhill 1750 -1894.
Charles McNicoll	Maryhill from 1895 - 1969: typescript.
Jean Lindsay	The Canals of Scotland: David and Charles, 1968.
Aileen Smart	Villages of Glasgow Vol.1: John Donald Publishers Ltd., 1988.
Woodside and North Kelvin Local History Project	From a Needle to an Anchor: Maryhill Community Central Hall, 1986
	Partick Thistle, The People's Club: Maryhill Community Central Hall, 1986.
	Scotland's Grand Canal, The Glasgow Branch of the Forth and Clyde: Crown Copyright, 1988.
Maryhill Historical Review Group	The Maryhill Directory and Historical Review, 1989.
Patrick Beaver	The Match Makers: Henry Melland, 1985.
John Emmet Farrell	The Universe is Mine, 1993.
W.A.C. Smith and Paul Anderson	An Illustrated History of Glasgow's Railways: Irwell Press, 1993.
T Louden	The Cinemas of Cinema City: The author, 1983.

ACKNOWLEDGEMENTS

The first people I must thank for helping me are the people of Maryhill, not just for their helpfulness, but also for the kindness with which they accepted me, an interloper from the other side of the river. They never made me feel like one.

I am grateful to Mr Wright, Mrs Scott and Mrs McCreadie of East Park Home for the pictures on pages 42, 43 and the back cover; Harry Elliot and Tommy Steedman of the Maryhill Bowling Club and Sam Wallace for the picture on page 10; John Emmet Farrell of Maryhill Harriers and Gordon Porteous for the picture on page 28; David Holgate for the picture on page 39; Gordon Anderson of Maryhill Junior Football Club, Bill Ferrier of the Maryhill Fleet, John Madden, David Forrester, the late William Miller and his daughter Alice, and Helen Vincent; Robert Reid and Partick Thistle Football Club for the picture on page 53; Derek Iggo of Maryhill Community Central Halls for access to the records of the Woodside and North Kelvin Local History Project and the pictures on pages 18 and 51; Father Willie Mone of the Church of the Immaculate Conception and Mrs Douglas Jay for the pictures on pages 11,19 and 31; the Rev. Ian MacKenzie of Gairbraid Church for the pictures on pages 24 and 27; Major Shaw and the staff of the Royal Highland Fusiliers Regimental Museum, for the pictures on the inside cover and pages 32, 33, and 34; George Robin for the picture on page 8; and Peter Stewart for the pictures on pages 2,15, 44, 45, and 46 (the three of Maryhill Road come from a montage taken in the late 1950's which themselves would make a fascinating publication).

Librarians and archivists are always enormously helpful and unfailingly cheerful and I must thank the staff of; Maryhill Library; the Glasgow Room of the Mitchell Library for the pictures on pages 8, 14, 40, 22, 23, and 52 (the first picture is from the G.H. Robin collection and the last three are from the John Logan Collection); Strathclyde Regional Archives for the pictures on pages 20 and 30; Hackney Archives, Roselipman Library, London and Bryant and May for the pictures on pages 36 and 37; Strathkelvin District Libraries for the picture on page 1.

George Waugh's photographic assistance has been invaluable. I am grateful too for the picture on page 12 and to Stenlake Publishing who 'found' the pictures on the front cover and pages 4, 5, 6, 9, 13, 16, 21, 26, 41, 47, 48, 49, 54 and 55.